SOLIHULL LODGE
The Victorian Years

SOLIHULL LODGE

The Victorian Years

by
S. Keith Adams

BREWIN BOOKS

First published
by Brewin Books, Studley, Warwickshire, B80 7LG
in September 1995

(c) S. Keith Adams 1995

All rights reserved.

ISBN 185858 057 9

British Library Cataloguing in Publication Data.
A Catalogue record for this book is available
from the British Library.

Typeset in Baskerville and
made and printed by
Supaprint (Redditch) Ltd

THE AUTHOR

Keith Adams was born and brought up in Shirley, Solihull, Warwickshire. When he married he and his wife set up home in Solihull Lodge and they still live in the area.

Educated at Sharmans Cross Secondary Modern School he has recently been awarded a Bachelor of Arts Degree, with Honours, by the Open University. It was during his university studies that he developed a keen interest in history, especially in Roman Britain and Local History. His decision to write this book was born out of his research into the history of Solihull Lodge the results of which he believes should be recorded.

Peacock Cottage, High Street, Solihull Lodge. C. Solihull Library.

CONTENTS

1.	Setting the Scene.	1
2.	Roads, Canals and the Railway.	4
3.	Farms and Related Industries.	10
4.	The Corn Mills.	17
5.	The Needle Industry.	23
6.	Houses and Cottages.	26
7.	Aluminium Works.	34
8.	Local Brickworks.	39
9.	The Solihull Lodge Community.	41
10.	Into the Twentieth Century.	49

The Windmill, Solihull Lodge. C. Solihull Library.

SETTING THE SCENE

Solihull Lodge, in the Metropolitan Borough of Solihull, is a portion of the ecclesiastical parish of Shirley situated between the River Cole and the boundaries of Birmingham and Hereford and Worcester.

The geology of the area is fairly simple, being covered by a layer of reddish-brown clay called Keuper marl. Large quantities of drift material comprising Boulder clay, stones, sand and gravel were deposited over the Keuper marl by glaciers during the Ice Age. When the ice melted the majority of these deposits were washed away but large quantities remained west of the Cole.

In the nineteenth-century probably the most significant natural resource which the area possessed was the River Cole. Its source is at Red Hill in Worcestershire and it travels 25 miles before it joins the River Blythe. When seen today it seems almost unbelievable that in Victorian times the Cole provided power for around thirteen water-mills, whilst its tributaries, of which the Peterbrook is one, powered another eight or nine. Two of these mills were located in Solihull Lodge.

The earliest evidence of the area being inhabited is undoubtedly provided by Berry Mound, an eleven acre Iron Age Hill Fort with banks and ditches, overlooking the River Cole and Peterbrook, which has been dated at around the first century BC.

How the area got its name is uncertain but one plausible explanation may be found in the adjustment of the parish and county boundaries, which took place around 1243. The reasons for the adjustment are not clear but it may have been to reward, with a parcel of land, the Lord of the Manor of Solihull, William d'Odingsell, for his devotion to the King. In this way Solihull secured a lodgement in the crown lands of Worcestershire, the new territory becoming known as Solihull Lodge.

The area is described in a survey of Solihull Manor dated 1632 as 'common or waste ground called Solihull Wood, by estimation 150 acres in extent'. It appears to have partly remained common land until the early nineteenth century when it was enclosed. Evidence to support that this is the case is provided by a reference to Solihull Lodge Common in a Rate Book of 1806. Indentures relating to Colebrook Priory Mill dated 1711 and 1747 also contain references to 'the common there called Solihull Wood'.

Today's traveller passing through the area would find it difficult to imagine that less than a hundred years ago it was a busy but sparsely populated farming area. It was, in the nineteenth century, an area of meadows, pastures, narrow country lanes, fords, mills both wind and water, beerhouses and both large residences and small cottages. At other times there was also a needle mill and an aluminium factory, whilst brickmaking continued throughout the period.

In the centuries preceding the Second World War the principle occupations available to the inhabitants were in farming or related trades, for example millers, blacksmiths and wheelwrights. The second half of the nineteenth century, however, saw alternative work opportunities offer themselves albeit for comparatively short periods of time.

It was not until after the Second World War that residential development gained pace resulting in the urban sprawl we know today.

In this book I hope to give the reader an impression of what Solihull Lodge would have been like between 1837 and 1891.

KEY:

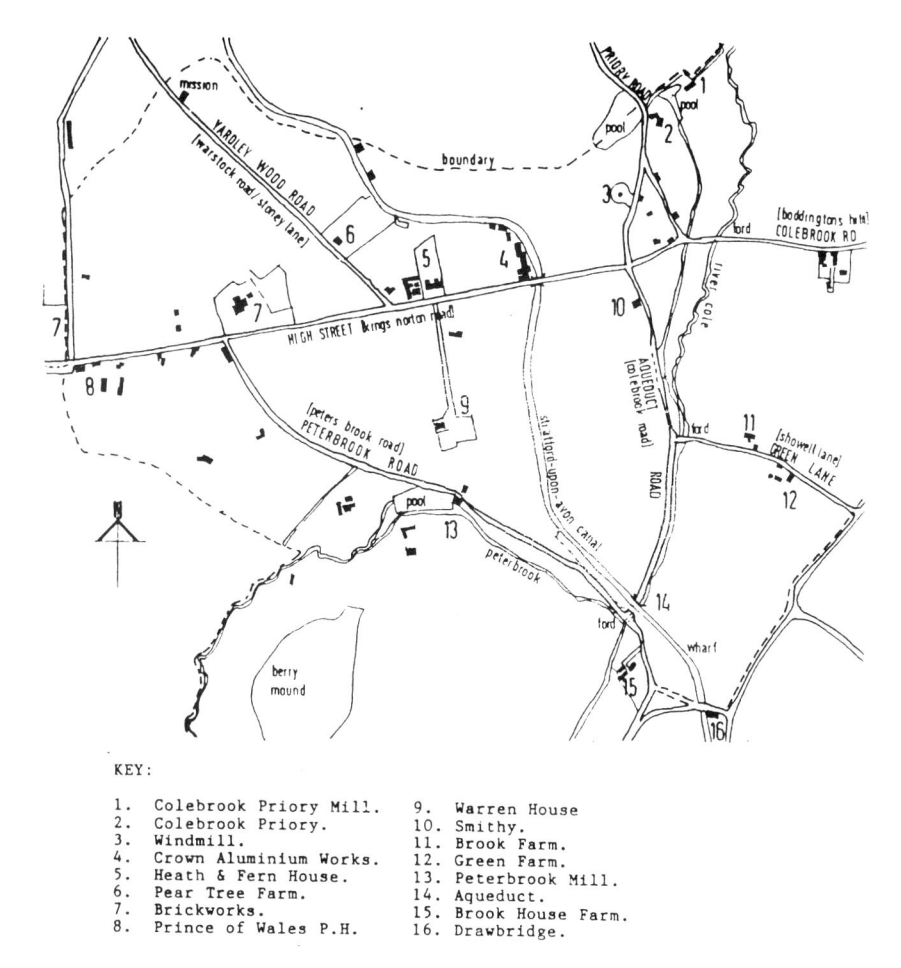

1. Colebrook Priory Mill.
2. Colebrook Priory.
3. Windmill.
4. Crown Aluminium Works.
5. Heath & Fern House.
6. Pear Tree Farm.
7. Brickworks.
8. Prince of Wales P.H.
9. Warren House
10. Smithy.
11. Brook Farm.
12. Green Farm.
13. Peterbrook Mill.
14. Aqueduct.
15. Brook House Farm.
16. Drawbridge.

Map 1. Principal Roads and features of Solihull Lodge. Based on 1905, 6in to 1 mile, Ordnance Survey Map with the kind permission of Ordnance Survey.

ROADS, CANALS AND THE RAILWAY

The roads which served Solihull Lodge in the nineteenth century were, in the main, those which exist today. In this earlier period, however, they were narrow leafy lanes not the broad expanse of tarmac, carrying great volumes of traffic, which we know today. It is not only the appearance of the roads which have changed over the decades, many have also been renamed.

In the Inclosure award of 1843 the High Street was a turnpike road referred to as Kings Norton Road whilst Peterbrook Road was Peters Brook Road. At this time Prince of Wales Lane did not exist as a public highway although a private carriageway or drift road followed roughly the same line as today's road.

The Award contained descriptions of the other roads which served the area at that date. Aqueduct Road was called Colebrook Road 'starting at the Aqueduct and running north over Solihull Lodge Common to Kings Norton Road into Yardley Wood at Bampton's Pool (Colebrook Priory Millpool). The small portion of this old road later became Priory Road before taking on its present name of Windmill Road. Yardley Wood Road was called Warstock Road 'starting at Yardley Wood Common to Kings Norton Road'. Later in the century it was known as Stoney Lane.

1

Aqueduct Road. A typical example of the 'leafy lanes' which served the area in the nineteenth century. Date unknown.

Finally the short stretch of Priory Road from Windmill Road to Colebrook Road was at one time called Colebrook Lane and the hill in Colebrook Road, which now takes vehicles under the railway bridge, was once known as Boddington's Hill, after the owner of Colebrook Hall Farm.

In addition to the changes in road names alterations have taken place to accommodate the growth in road transport.

In the nineteenth century the River Cole was crossed by fords in Peterbrook Road at the Aqueduct, in Green Lane and in Colebrook Road. At all of these fords pedestrians were able to cross the river by means of a footbridge but during heavy winter rains the river was liable to flood, as occurs at the Aqueduct today. Consequently the fords were impassable, even to pedestrians using the footbridges, and as a result Solihull Lodge would have been cut off from the village of Shirley. With the development of road transport all of the fords were eventually bridged, and in the case of Green Lane the road was totally realigned to make Aqueduct Road and Green Lane into a continuous carriageway.

The ford where the River Cole crossed Green Lane near it's junction with Aqueduct Road. The timber pedestrian bridge is also shown. pre 1938.

Green Lane, which was considered to be in Solihull Lodge in Census returns, was also altered at its junction with Haslucks Green Road. This was brought about by the construction of the railway bridge. For many years the line of the original hedge could still be traced on the site now occupied by Shirley Evangelical Church.

A narrow hump-backed bridge once carried people using the High Street over the Stratford-upon-Avon Canal. This was replaced in 1962/1963 by the present road bridge.

An important influence on nineteenth century Solihull Lodge was undoubtedly the Stratford-upon-Avon Canal. Conceived in the eighteenth century, an Act of Parliament was passed in 1793 authorising a capital outlay of £200,000 with authority to raise an additional £60,000. Building began in November 1793.

The objective behind the building of the canal was to link Stratford-upon-Avon with Birmingham and the coal mines and factories of the industrial Midlands. It was seen as providing a means of transporting goods, such as coal from the Midlands and corn from Stratford, which could not easily be moved over the existing turnpike roads.

Work began at the northern end where it joined the Worcester and Birmingham Canal at Kings Norton. The excavation was undertaken using pick and shovel for which the contractor was paid at a rate of between 5d and 5½d per cubic yard. The stretch of the canal from Kings Norton to Hockley Heath was constructed at a consistent level and no locks were therefore required. Two of the features which presented the engineers with their greatest challenge on this length of the canal were situated in Solihull Lodge. These were the Solihull Common embankment and the brick built aqueduct over the River Cole. A short distance from the aqueduct the road was carried over the canal by means of a 'lift bridge', originally constructed of timber, its modern day replacement being not dissimilar in appearance. There is no evidence as to why this type of crossing was chosen but, as money became short, it would seem reasonable to assume that it was the cheapest available option.

3

The Aqueduct which carries the Stratford-upon-Avon Canal over Aqueduct Road and the River Cole. 1995.

4

The Drawbridge showing the lift bridge with the Drawbridge Stores and Inn to the left. The rowing boat suggests the canal was used for leisure as well as commercial purposes in the nineteenth century.

Despite the apparent lack of major construction problems by the time the work reached Hockley Heath the available money had been spent. The completed length of canal was opened for business on 25th. May, 1796 but it was not until 24th. June, 1816 that the fully completed canal came into service.

There is a considerable amount of evidence available to support the idea that the existence of the canal had an important bearing on the community of the area during the nineteenth century. Cottages, beerhouses and industrial buildings were all sited adjacent to it, suggesting that it was well used. It is also evident that some residents found employment on the canal, George Sale Senior and William Walker described themselves in the 1871 census as boatmen, as did Alfred Sale, aged 15, in 1881.

An entry in the Tythe Apportionment of 1837, together with those in the Census Enumerators Books of 1841/51, inform us that a Mary Kite and her husband John lived in a Canal Side Cottage, situated between the High Street bridge and Yardley Wood. They described themselves as Beerhouse Keepers. The same sources also confirm that James Payton, who was at Pear Tree Farm in Yardley Wood Road, also ran a Beerhouse adjacent to the canal. It would seem to be a reasonable assumption that moorings were provided to allow the canal users to avail themselves of the facilities offered. This was certainly the case at the Drawbridge and remains so today. The Ordnance Survey map dated 1883 appears to indicate a small 'basin' off the canal near to Pear Tree Farm but what it was used for is uncertain.

There is evidence of the existence of licensed premises at the Drawbridge, also known as the Boatmans Rest, from as early as 1841. It has been suggested that the canal towpath was an 'open air taproom'. It was also frequently called the 'Drawbridge Stores' with several of the occupiers, Thomas Woodward in 1851/61 and Edmund Field in 1881 being described as coal dealers. I assume that those trading in coal had supplies delivered to the nearby canal wharf to transport it by road to households in the locality. The wharf would have been used to onload goods from the local mills for transportation into Birmingham.

Towards the end of the nineteenth century the Stratford-upon-Avon Canal witnessed a decline in use as a major means of transporting goods, a situation brought about by the developing railway systems. Canals were at the mercy of the elements which resulted in their being unreliable, not only during winter months, when they froze up, but also during hot summer periods, when they dried up.

This is explicit in a speech, promoting the virtues of railways, made by one William James. James suggested that,

> '..*moving vehicles on railroads by steam engines can be done cheaper, more certain and twice as expeditiously, as by boat on navigable canals, and neither the repairs of locks and banks, the want of water, the summers heat or winters frost, will retard the operation'. (Hadfield)*

In 1845 the Great Western Railway and their financiers planned to construct a railway from Birmingham to Moreton and Cheltenham, passing through Stratford-upon-Avon. As part of this plan they offered to purchase the Stratford-upon-Avon Canal.

It appears that the original plan was to build the railway on the line of the canal. The Stratford-upon-Avon shareholders described the agreement as, '*....for the sale of this canal for the purpose of converting same into a Railway for Locomotive Carriages'. (Hadfield)* This proposal was not of course implemented and the Birmingham to Stratford line was built nearby and eventually opened in 1907. What is unusual is that approximately fifty years prior to the opening of the Stratford line a family was living in a railway carriage near to the Aqueduct. In 1891 two engine drivers, James Sale and Alfred Bartlett lived in the area. They could have worked on either the Great Western or Midland Railways.

The opening of the railway from Birmingham to Stratford-upon-Avon led to the canal falling into disuse and disrepair until the Stratford-upon-Avon Canal Society was formed in 1956 when local enthusiasts began its renovation.

FARMS AND RELATED INDUSTRIES

Prior to the twentieth century the vast majority of the land in Solihull Lodge was devoted to farming and related industries.

From the Tythe Map of 1837 we can see the uses to which the land was put. In general terms these could be grouped into three areas. Not surprisingly most of the land skirting the River Cole was meadow and mown grass, which was grazed. South of Peterbrook Road it was arable, meadow and pasture and finally in the triangle formed by High Street, Peterbrook Road and Aqueduct Road, arable and seeds with a few plots of potatoes.

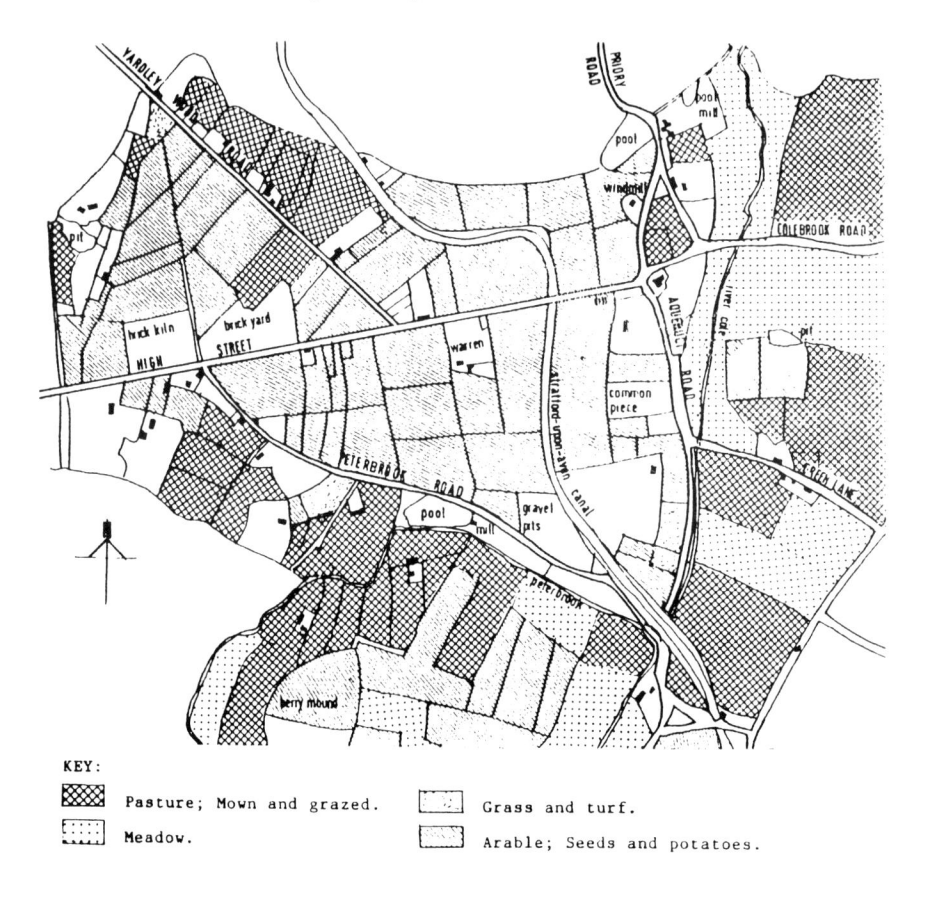

KEY:
- Pasture; Mown and grazed.
- Meadow.
- Grass and turf.
- Arable; Seeds and potatoes.

Map 2. *Principal land uses in 1837. Based on the Tythe Map of 1837.*

The field names used in the Tythe apportionment also provide an aid to developing a picture of the area as some indicate the nature of the land, its location or use. Names like Rushy Meadow, Rushy Close and Rushy Piece, found near to the Cole, suggest that the land was naturally wet and perhaps boggy. Other parcels of land were known for their natural habitat or crops grown, Thistly Piece, Clover Close and Oat Close being typical examples. Others such as Canal Close, Bridge Close, Brook Close and Canal Piece bore names related to their location. Finally, titles such as Brick-kiln pits, Warren Close and Common Turf appear to relate to the use to which the land was put.

One of the most common occupations for men during the nineteenth century was that of farm labourer. In 1841 twenty-six people in Solihull Lodge described themselves as being employed in this role. At that time, however, there were only four farmers in the area and it would seem that many of the labourers would have had to walk several miles to their place of work on neighbouring farms. The numbers of farm labourers in the area peaked in 1861 and then decreased as the century progressed. In 1851 there were twenty two, 1861 thirty three, 1871 nineteen, 1881 twelve and in 1891 the number was down to seven. This was in keeping with the national trend which saw the numbers of agricultural labourers decline during the nineteenth century. Countrywide, in 1851 approximately a quarter of employed men worked on farms but by 1901 this figure had reduced by half. There were various reasons for this decline in numbers, the availability of cheaper imported wheat, an agricultural depression between 1875 and 1895 and developments in farm machinery, being examples. Added to these was the temptation of higher wages in the fast growing factories of the industrial towns.

Wages for agricultural labourers varied between areas ranging from a low of 8 shillings a week (40 pence) to as much as 20 shillings (£1). Some were still paid in kind with free beer, cider or potatoes. Following riots in the 1830s and 1870s, Joseph Arch formed the National Agricultural Labourers Union in 1872. By 1874 wages had increased by between 1 and 3 shillings a week.

In the 1870s the size of the average farm in the north and west of England was around 70 acres and employed 2 or 3 labourers. Farms in the south were somewhat larger, averaging about 100 acres and employing 5 or 6 labourers. In 1871 of the farms in Solihull Lodge only a small number conformed to the national pattern, the remainder were much smaller averaging only 22½ acres.

During the reign of Queen Victoria there were four farms named in the census in Solihull Lodge. They were Green Farm and

Brook Farm situated in Green Lane, Brookhouse Farm, sometimes called Aqueduct Farm, in Peterbrook Road and Pear Tree Farm in Yardley Wood Road. The information contained in the Census Enumerators Books suggests that there were also several smaller farms.

The number of farmers in the area followed a similar pattern to that of farm labourers. In 1841 the number was four which increased in 1851 to eleven, peaked in 1861 at twelve before reducing to six in 1871 and seven in both 1881 and 1891.

Green Farm was located in Green Lane opposite its junction with Cole Green. The farm house was set at right angles to the road with the farm outbuildings following the road boundary. It is said that it was given its name in about 1433 by Sir Thomas Green of the Guild of Knowle.

The original farm house was, in the twentieth century, replaced by a new building nearby which was used for a time, prior to its demolition, as a doctors' surgery.

The land which belonged to Green Farm was between Green Lane and the canal, that which is now occupied by the housing estate entered by Mappleborough Road, and was described as being 'meadow and pasture'. The area of land which was adjacent to the River Cole was wet and marshy and would not, therefore, have been suitable for any other use.

In 1837 it was owned by Thomas Salmon and farmed by Richard Biddle. Information from the census informs us that in 1871 and 1881 the occupier was John Howard, a farm bailiff, and that by 1891 Charles Upton had become the farmer.

Almost directly opposite to Green Farm was Brook Farm, the site of which is now occupied by the Coronation Youth Club building.

Brook Farm was also known as Showell Farm in 1861, when Green Lane was called Showell Lane. The name Brook would have most probably derived from its close proximity to the River Cole.

Brook Farm was demolished in around 1938 to make way for the construction of the Cole Green council estate. The estate was not built, however, until after the Second World War. Some of the fields which made up the farm and have now been developed as playing fields were for a number of years used as a refuse tip.

Much of the farm's land, like that of its neighbour Green Farm, was used as meadow and pasture although some of the fields were put to arable use. The nature of the land would have been very much the same as that of its near neighbour Green Farm.

Brook Farm in Green Lane

Lack of definite addresses on the census returns make it difficult to determine precisely who was farming the land during some of the Victorian period. It is known, however, that John Warboys was the tenant farmer in 1841 and at that time it was owned by Elizabeth Warboys. By the time of the 1881 census Thomas Clift, a cattle dealer, was in occupation. He had left by 1891 and been replaced by Arthur Cook.

Records tell us that in 1861 John Kite, who kept a beerhouse by the canal in 1841/51, was a farmer in Showell Lane, as was his son Thomas. The available evidence, therefore, suggests that they may have been tenants of Green Farm and Brook Farm. John farmed 80 acres employing two men and a boy. He died at the ripe old age of 82 in 1878.

The similarity between the names of Brook Farm and Brook House Farm, which was located near to the Aqueduct, can present difficulties when carrying out research into the area. These difficulties are compounded by another Brook House Farm located near to Berry Mound.

Brook House Farm, also known during the nineteenth century as Aqueduct Farm, and today called Brook House lies back from Peterbrook Road opposite the Aqueduct.

Measuring between 80 and 100 acres it was one of the larger farms in the district and, like others nearby, its fields were used for arable or for meadow and pasture.

Owned by Issac Anderton in 1837 it was farmed by Joseph Guest. In 1851 William Amos was farming 100 acres there, helped by a servant and three farm labourers. He had a wife Lydia and two daughters.

William had died by 1861 when Lydia was described as a widow but was then using the surname of Herrins which may have been her maiden name. By that date she had three sons and was farming 90 acres with the help of a farm bailiff and a cowman.

Ten years later Lydia, still farming at the Aqueduct, had married John Mace who was many years her junior. Her children were at this time referred to as 'in-laws' and bore the surname Herrins. The size of the farm was said to be 80 acres and they employed one man and a boy.

By 1881 the acreage had shrunk to 47 acres and only one man helped on the farm. John was not at home on the night of the census but Lydia had her daughter Mary Ann and grandson Baron, aged 10, living with her. Her grandson was recorded as being 'dumb from birth'.

The Mace family do not appear on the 1891 census. William Gee was recorded as farming Brook House Farm but whether this was at the Aqueduct or Berry Mound is not clear.

It is claimed that in 1900 Brook House Farm suffered a set back when the canal overflowed resulting in the farm animals being up their necks in water.

The fourth main farm in the area, situated in Yardley Wood Road, adjacent to the canal, was Pear Tree Farm. This farm, however, differed from the others in that it was used, not only as a farm, but also as a beerhouse. It is said that it was also known at one time as 'The White Lion'.

James Payton lived at Pear Tree Farm with his wife Mary, one daughter and three sons, two of whom became Railway Contractors. The farm at 27 acres was only small, but, in 1841, James Payton was still able to employ an agricultural labourer who 'lived in', and by the time of the 1851 census he employed two house servants, aged 16 and 14 years respectively. There is no way of telling for sure but this suggests that the combination of farm and beerhouse proved to be a profitable one. In later years the beerhouse was closed and tenants concentrated on farming. During the period between 1891 and 1900 William Clarke, a widower, occupied the farm with his two young daughters. He was a Dairy man, who may have supplied milk to the area, and he was able to employ two servants, one of whom was a housekeeper.

In an area chiefly devoted to farming it was usual to find allied industries or trades which served the needs of the local community. Solihull Lodge was no exception possessing corn mills, discussed in a later chapter, blacksmiths, wheelwrights, carriers and carters.

A blacksmith was an essential member of every agricultural community. He was responsible for the making and fitting of horseshoes, the repair of farming tools and implements, wrought iron work and tyring of cart wheels.

Pear Tree Farm which used to be situated in Yardley Wood Road.

The first blacksmith recorded in the area, on the 1841 census, was John Warden but he had been replaced by 1845 by Solihull born William Fox, described in 1851 as a 'home forger'. Records show that he also made coach harness furniture and was wealthy enough to employ a servant. He rented land in Aqueduct Road from John Warboys and when he died of 'decay' in 1860 aged 74 was succeeded by his son George. Goerge lived with his mother and was described as a jobbing smith, wheelwright and blacksmith. George is unusual in that the evidence suggests that after the death of his wife Harriet in 1864 at the age of 64 he re-married. His new wife's name was Rosanna. He had no children and as a consequence there was no one to inherit the business. We find that by 1891 the smithy was occupied by William Roberts.

William Roberts worked the smithy in Aqueduct Road living nearby in a house called 'The Glains'. It is possible that this house is still there but if so it has been greatly renovated and altered. William came from Buckinghamshire and he and his wife Elizabeth had four sons, one of whom, William junior, took over the business. William junior was known to locals as 'Bumper Roberts'.

Wheelwrights made and repaired wheels for carriages and farm carts and records show that, including George Fox, four operated in the area during the Victorian period. In 1861 forty year old Charles Lewis, living at Canal Side described himself as a wheelwright, as did Charles Crathorne. The 1871 census does not include Lewis but Charles Crathorne remained and a new wheelwright, Joseph Hall, was living in the area.

The skills of Blacksmiths and Wheelwrights were vital to a farming community and this was reflected in the ability of a journeyman in 1890 to earn as much as thirty shillings a week. (£1.50).

Another group, whose services were essential in a community, were the carters and carriers. With their horse-drawn carts they transported farm and mill produce and delivered household goods. In 1871 these services were provided by James Shipton, a common carrier and James Quiney, a carter. The only carter recorded in 1881 was George Sale. Ten years later Harry Tillsley, a waggoner and Richard Birch a horse carter, served the area whilst Richard Taylor, living at Colebrook Priory, provided the specialist service of miller's carter. His wagon would probably have been recognisable by its canvas tilt.

THE CORN MILLS

During the reign of Queen Victoria there were three corn mills operating in the Solihull Lodge area. Peterbrook and Priory Mills were powered by water, the third was Solihull Lodge Windmill.

The earliest reference I have found to Peterbrook Water Mill is in the Tythe Apportionment of 1837 which states that Issac Anderton owned and occupied the Oatmeal Mill, Pools etc, plot number 2441, whilst the outbuildings and pasture croft were occupied by Thomas Bird.

It obtained its power from a mill race fed from the Peterbrook. A head race was formed, with an aqueduct constructed to carry it over the brook. It fed a mill pool, which can still be seen today, situated alongside Peterbrook Road. The tail race then carried water to rejoin the Peterbrook before it joined the Cole at the Aqueduct.

The building which occupied the site in 1843 was said to be of a cruck frame construction infilled with small bricks. This type of construction suggests that the building may have dated back as far as the sixteenth century or even earlier.

The Census Enumerator's Book of 1841 indicates that one Thomas Avery, a 40 year old miller, occupied the mill with his wife Anne. By the time of the 1851 census, however, the mill had been taken over by Joseph Else who lived there with his wife Jane and their family. It is worthy of note to mention here that both Joseph and Jane were born in Derbyshire, he in Ashover and she in Aldwork, and thus provide evidence that people were prepared to travel considerable distances from their birthplace to find work. At the time of the 1851 census Joseph described himself as a farmer and miller, but ten years later he had changed this description to read master miller.

An entry in Kelly's Trade Directory of 1884 refers to Joseph Else as being a Steam and Water miller confirming that the mill was, in the latter half of the nineteenth century, converted to operate on steam power. This evidence is further supported by a photograph of Peterbrook Road which clearly shows the mill to have a large chimney stack. It continued to be referred to as a Steam and Water Mill well into the twentieth century. In 1891 Joseph's son, John George was living and working at the mill, with his father, his wife Sarah and their daughter.

*Peterbrook Oatmeal Mill in Peterbrook Road.
The tall chimney stack suggests it was converted
from water to steam power.*

Joseph Else remained at the mill until his death in 1894 at the age of 87 years. Both he and his wife who died in 1890, aged 66 years, are buried in St. James Churchyard in Shirley.

Until the 1950s it was possible to find evidence of where the mill wheel once stood. Sadly all traces of the building have now disappeared leaving only the millpool as a reminder of the past.

Solihull Lodge Windmill was situated on high ground in Windmill Road overlooking the Cole Valley near to Colebrook Priory and Bamptons Millpool.

The building which occupied the site during the nineteen century was a brick tower mill. A brief description of the mill is to be found in the 1845 Directory of Solihull which refers to Kendrick's Mill as 'a three storey tower mill about fifty feet high'. A fourth storey and an ogee cap complete with weather cock was added later in the nineteenth century. The mill was powered by four double shuttered sails which drove three pairs of millstones, a bean splitter, an oat crusher and driving gear.

It is possible that the nineteenth century mill was preceded by a timber post mill similar to that from Danzy Green which can be seen today at the Avoncroft Museum at Bromsgrove.

The Windmill in Windmill Lane viewed across Bamptons Pool in the nineteenth century.

Bamptons Pool as it is today looking towards where the windmill used to be.

The Tythe of 1837 states that John Kendrick, who was related to Mary Bampton of the Priory, owned and occupied the windmill plot and windmill. Kendrick's ownership is further confirmed by an entry in the Solihull Enclosure Act of 1843 when it refers to 'Mrs Booth's Mill Pool beyond Kendrick's Mill'. It is very likely that prior to 1837 the mill was owned by John Kendrick's father Joseph.

Records show that the windmill remained in the ownership of the Kendrick family until 1885.

In 1841 John Kendrick was the miller and he occupied a nearby house with his wife Elizabeth, three daughters and son John junior who was also a miller. It can only be assumed that at some time during the next ten years John senior died because by 1851 John junior had taken over. He had his three sisters and Edwin Lea, described at this time as a servant but later as a nephew, living with him.

The relationship of Edwin Lea to John Kendrick is important because in 1881 Edwin in partnership with his brother Thomas were described as working the mill.

The windmill ceased to be operated by the Kendrick family in 1885 when Edwin Lea leased it to a miller, Nathan Bradford Woollaston for seven years at a rent of £60 per annum. The legal documents relating to this transaction describe the windmill as being void at this time which is possible, as it is known that in 1883 Thomas Lea was using the nearby Colebrook Priory Mill, which is discussed below.

In the twentieth century the windmill remained unused for many years before it was eventually blown up in 1957 to allow the development of the Coton Grove housing estate. Much later Kendrick's house was also demolished and Wishaw Close was constructed on the site.

Colebrook Priory Mill was situtated adjacent to the River Cole at the rear of the house known today as Colebrook Priory. It was first recorded in the Boundary Presentment of 1495 when it was referred to as Bache Mill, Bache meaning 'land by a stream'. It retained this name into the eighteenth century and appears as such on Beighton's Map of 1725.

Surviving documents do confirm that the mill and the house were transferred from one owner to another as a complete package. The property is described in an Indenture dated 1711 as:

> *'...that messuage ffarm or tenement and all*
> *of that water corn mill with bridges, banking,*
> *floodgates, waters, watercourses pools and*
> *ponds, fish and fishing to the said water mill*

adjoining belonging or appertaining and the majority of the barns, stable buildings, gardens .....the land ..... situate lying and being in Solihull in the said county of Warwick between the land there called Colebrook Lane ...... the common there called Solihull Wood .....'

Colebrook Priory Mill. c1913.

    The mill was, however, often leased and worked by a tenant who did not occupy the house.

    Photographic records suggest that the mill building comprised a simple two storey brick construction which obtained its power from the River Cole.

    The waters of the Cole were harnessed to provide sufficient quantities and control to power a successful milling operation. The head race began just to the north of the Green Lane ford and, having travelled along the rear boundaries of the present houses in Aqueduct Road, passed under the High Street to eventually feed a small mill pool. A short tail race was then constructed to rejoin the Cole. Traces of the head race can still be seen today along the boundary between the public open space and properties in Aqueduct Road. It is especially noticeable adjacent to the High Street.

The contents of a Lease dated 1829 state that the mill contained, '..2 overshot wheels ....3 pairs of French stones (French Buhr made the finest stones).... 1 pair of Derby Stones, 2 flour machines, sack tackle and so forth'.

In 1799 it was owned by Joseph Kendrick, who you will recall also owned the nearby windmill, and he leased it to one William Dester. By 1816 the property had passed into the ownership of Mary Booth, Joseph Kendrick's daughter, and it was she who first leased it for use as a Needle Mill which is discussed in the next chapter. The tenant in 1829 was John Austin Bampton, Mary Booth's son-in-law. During the nineteenth century the tenancy of the mill changed hands quite frequently but the ownership appears to have remained within the same family for much of the period.

At the beginning of the 1850's it reverted to being used as a corn mill with Thomas Lea, Kendrick's nephew, who operated the windmill, as tenant.

In 1883 John Woollaston leased the mill from John Bampton's son Richard Bampton. It is interesting to note that as part of the lease agreement John Woollaston was required to provide:

> '..a stable for 2 horses, cart shed and office,
> a privy, ... and to keep in working order the
> mill, mill grinding gear and machinery, mill dam,
> floodgates, brickwork and other works to the mill'.

From time to time, the millstones became worn and required the furrows to be re-chipped, a process called 'dressing'. This task may have been undertaken by John Woollaston himself but it is possible that a millwright might have been employed who would also have constructed and repaired mill machinery. There is evidence of one wheerwright residing in the area in 1881.

The last person to own and work Priory Mill was Nathan Bradford Woollaston, son of John, who lived at Colebrook Priory. Colebrook Priory Mill ceased to operate in about 1919 when the Woollaston family opened a new roller mill in Haslucks Green Road near to Shirley Station.

The water mill was demolished, and its pool filled in, to make way for the building of Nethercote Gardens in 1965. Bampton's Pool opposite the Priory, which remains today, was only used as an additional feeder pool for the mill, if needed, its main purpose being a fishing pool.

THE NEEDLE INDUSTRY

The seventeenth century saw the needle industry move from London to become established in and around the Worcestershire town of Redditch. At first this took the form of a Cottage Industry which developed between 1700 and 1800 into a factory system.

This industry was surprisingly found in Solihull Lodge when, for a period of something like fifteen years in the middle of the nineteenth century, the Colebrook Priory Corn Mill was used for the manufacture of needles. The first needle maker to use the mill, recorded in the Tythe of 1837, was John Austin Bampton.

In 1839 the mill was leased by John Bampton's wife Mary to a Samuel Roberts of Redditch in the County of Worcester, needle manufacturer and fish hook maker, for a period of twenty one years at a rent of £120 per year. He had an option to draw water from the pool opposite the Priory. A clause in his lease stated:

> '... if the said Samuel Roberts should put up an additional wheel for drilling or blue pointing he may draw off water from such pool for working such wheel not lowering the water more than twelve inches below the present pool gate, near the said road and so as not to injure the fish in such pool'.

The census returns for 1841 and 1851 confirm that Samuel Roberts was at the Priory and he is described in White's Directory of Warwickshire 1850 as a Needle Manufacturer at Priory Mill. The entry in the census of 1851 describes him as 'employer of 110 hands, maker of needles and fishhooks'. Many of these employees may have worked from home. In 1841 fifteen needle workers lived in the Solihull Lodge area a figure which had increased to 31 in 1851. This latter figure represented approximately 18.5% of the population over the age of ten, against whom an occupation was entered in the census returns. It is interesting to note that in 1841 half of those employed in the industry were aged 15 or younger, the youngest being only 10 years old. The work force were slightly older by 1851 when 6 were 15 years old or younger, 2 were aged 40 or over and the remainder in their 20s.

The Indenture between Samuel Roberts and Mary Bampton contained a fairly comprehensive schedule of equipment and machinery available for needle making at Colebrook Priory Mill. Included in the schedule were '...four pointing trams with guards .... dresser for eight blue pointers ....tempering stone....hardening hole...'. Comparison of this information with the knowledge we can glean from Forge Mill Museum shows that Colebrook Priory Mill was fully equipped as a needle mill except for the drying process. It also provides an indication of the jobs available to the local community at that time.

In 1841 the only job description provided was that of needle worker but the 1851 census provided more detailed descriptions of the jobs which some of the workers were employed to undertake. The census included a 'rough pointer' and three 'needle pointers' aged between 24 and 30 years.

The job of the needle pointer was probably the most dangerous in the industry and attracted the highest wages. In 1846 a needle pointer could earn as much as £4 per week whilst other workers received less than 10 shillings (50 pence). Holding 50 needles in his hands the pointer sat astride a bench which held a grinding stone turned by a pulley. He pointed the needles by placing them against the revolving stone. Sometimes the grind stone splintered causing serious, sometimes fatal, injuries. The pointer usually wore a scarf across his nose and mouth but this did not prevent the inhalation of dust and sparks. Inevitably this led to lung damage and a crippling diseased called 'Pointers Rot'. Few pointers lived beyond the age of thirty five years.

After pointing the needles were stamped to flatten the end to receive the eye, a process carried out by 'needle stampers' of which two, Joseph Stevens aged 18 and Andrew Dedicoat aged 26, lived in the area. The next stage was to form the eyes and there were two needle eyers, 16 year old Jacob Clarke and 17 year old John Stevens, recorded.

The jobs listed above would have been carried out in the mill premises because they required power to drive the necessary machinery. Other functions, however, may have been carried out in the home as a cottage industry, often by children.

The process known as stamping produced an area of excess metal around the eye of the needle. To enable this to be removed the double needles were threaded, or spitted, onto thin strips of metal called spits. This was a job usually done by women or children, the one spitter recorded was 12 year old Thomas Stevens. People must also have been employed as scourers and hardeners but there is no record of them living in Solihull Lodge.

During the 1840s and 50s Robert's Needle Mill provided the major source of employment outside agriculture for the residents of

Solihull Lodge and the adjoining areas. Of the 110 hands he employed in 1851 only a small proportion lived in Solihull Lodge.

It is noticeable that in some instances whole families were employed in the manufacture of needles. In 1841 John Dedicoat had two sons, Andrew and John and a daughter Diannah, all working in the industry. They were still making needles ten years later and had been joined by brothers Henry and Richard. Similar situations were to be found in the families of Mary Stevens whose three sons and a daughter all worked in the industry as did Charlotte Baxter's two sons and two daughters.

By the date of the 1861 census, however, all trace of a needle manufacturing industry, and almost all of those employed in it, including Samuel Roberts, had disappeared from the area. Those who remained were William Juggins and his wife Sarah who in 1861 describe themselves as an Agricultural Labourer and Laundress, and Dinah, the wife of Thomas Millward, who now described herself as a Laundress.

Samuel Roberts did not operate the needle mill for the full term of his lease, but why he ceased to trade and what happened to him, his family and most of his workers is a mystery.

HOUSES AND COTTAGES

The 'homestead' belonging to Colebrook Priory Mill is situated opposite Bamptons Pool in Priory Road. Its ownership has always been linked to that of the mill, although the millers did not necessarily live in the Priory.

Colebrook Priory.

How the house got its name is unknown as there is no documentary evidence that a priory ever occupied the site. Had there been it would most probably have served as a hostel for those travelling between Pershore Abbey and Maxstoke Priory. If such a building existed it would have been unlikely to have survived after the dissolution of the Abbey by Henry VIII in 1539. It has been suggested that an earth mound in the garden was a 'praying mound' once used by monks but there is no supporting evidence and its origin, like the house name, remains a mystery.

The original house has been much altered and the external facade belies its timber frame construction. The plan form also suggests that it was built with a 'cross passage'. This evidence suggests that whilst it is believed the house was built in the seventeenth century it may well date from even earlier.

The Priory did not stand alone, however. It had two cottages attached, one at the rear called Colebrook Priory Cottage and Colebrook Cottage to the side. The residential complex was completed by Fern Cottage which was located adjacent to the mill buildings.

Early in the nineteenth century the Kendrick family, who worked the windmill, owned the Priory. By 1837 it was in the ownership of Mary Booth, Joseph Kendrick's daughter. It is not clear how Mary Booth came by the property rather than her brother John Kendrick. We can only speculate that she inherited it on the death of her father or that she received it as a gift. It later passed to her daughter Mary Bampton and remained in the Bamptons' ownership for much of the remainder of the century but was occupied by various families.

In 1837 the occupants were Mary Booth's daughter, Mary, her husband John Austin Bampton and their family. By 1841 the census records the occupier of the Priory as being Samuel Roberts who was at that time working the Needle Mill. Ten years later it was again occupied by a member of the Bampton family. Mary's daughter Emma and son Richard Raphael were living there. On the day of the 1861 census Mary is recorded as being a visitor at the Priory and is described as a 'landed proprietor'. By 1881 Mary, now a widow, was living at the Priory with her son Richard and his wife Caroline.

The Bampton's ceased to occupy the house in 1889 when Richard Bampton leased it to Nathan Bradford Woollaston who eventually purchased the property. It is strange to note, however, that two years later it was occupied by a Richard Taylor, a millers carter. With this one exception members of the Woollaston family have occupied the Priory until the present day.

In 1861 Mary Bampton's daughter and son-in-law, Mary and Alfred Green were living on the Priory site, probably at Colebrook Cottage. Alfred was described as a Landscape and figure artist, whilst one of his eight children, fourteen year old Marion, was an artist of flowers.

The occupants of the cottages on the site are difficult to trace accurately but records show that in 1891 John Perrigo, a flour miller, and his family were the residents of Colebrook Priory Cottage.

The details of a lease dated 18th. June, 1889, relating to Colebrook Cottage, confirm that Richard Bampton let the property to a Thomas Smith for a period of 5 years, at an annual rent of £30 for the first year and £33 thereafter. The lease provided Thomas Smith with:

> *'...that messuage dwelling house or cottage situate at Solihull Lodge .... with the garden, outbuildings adjoining and the pleck of land (part whereof is covered by a pool of water) on the opposite side of the road....'*

It also bestowed upon him certain responsibilities:

> *'...to the best of his ability preserve fish in the said pool from being trespassed upon and will use the said pool in a sportsmanlike manner not netting or permitting the same to be netted for the capture of the fish therein but angling for the same with rod or trimmers only....'*

Thomas Smith described himself in the census of 1891 as letting the fishing pool. It is interesting to note that the pool is still let out for fishing today.

In 1881 it was recorded that Eliza Betts, a domestic housekeeper, and her family were living at the Needle Mill. The most logical interpretation of this information is that they lived in Fern Cottage. It would also seem logical that she was most probably employed at the Priory.

Another notable house in the area was Warren House. In 1837 the original house, which was situated off the High Street on land now occupied by Myton Drive was occupied by a Thomas Hastings and owned by the Honourable Elizabeth Musgrove.

Warren House probably derived its name from the rabbit warrens which occupied the site. In the middle ages areas of land were let to Warreners who bred rabbits as a commercial enterprise to provide meat and fur. Such areas of land were fenced off to protect the rabbits from predators such as foxes. The land in this locality would have been especially suitable for warrens as it is light and sandy in formation and thus well drained. An entry in the Tythe Apportionment of 1837 refers to 'Warren Close' and 'further Warren Close' located on the site. This is supported by an entry in the Inclosure award which states that '..Representatives of Christopher Musgrove Esq. deceased, retained rights to their rabbit warrens...'

By the time of the 1861 census the house was owned, and occupied, by the Chattock family. The Chattock family lived in Castle Bromwich for centuries, and they subsequently became one of the principal landowners in Shirley and Solihull.

They appear to have rebuilt the house siting it further back from the road but retaining the name of Warren House. In keeping with its importance a tree lined driveway, part of which can still be seen today in the grounds of Peterbrook School, led to the house.

The Avenue of trees in the grounds of Peterbrook Primary School which used to line the driveway to Warren House. 1995.

Thomas Percy Chattock, the head of the family in 1861 and described as a 'land proprietor and Civil Engineer', was born in Solihull whilst his wife Sarah Anne came from Yorkshire. According to the census returns they had eight children, four boys and four girls, all of whom were baptised at St. James Church in Shirley.

I will discuss the employment of domestic servants in a later chapter but it is worthy of note here that the Chattocks, for much of the Victorian period, employed a cook, housemaid and, whilst the children were young, a nursemaid, all living-in at the house.

Located near to the house were two cottages, Warren House Cottages, which would have most probably been used to house other employees. One of these was John Cross an agricultural labourer. He lived in one of the cottages with his wife Eliza, six sons, all of whom became agricultural labourers, and one daughter. John met an unfortunate end when in 1876, aged 66, he was killed by a kick from a horse. His son James continued to live at the cottage at least until 1891.

The other cottage in 1891 was occupied by George Fox who was described as a coachman and domestic servant, whilst his wife Sarah was a domestic servant and laundress. The employment of a coachman would have been in keeping with the social standing of the Chattock family.

Thomas Percy Chattock died, at the of 57, in 1880 and was buried in St. James Churchyard. Sarah, his wife, continued to live at Warren House until her death in 1911.

Also situated in the High Street was Fern House which was probably built around 1876 by James Fern Webster, whose inventive talents and connections with aluminium are discussed later. It was one half of a large semi-detached property, the other half being called Heath House. Both houses occupied the site on which stands Lichfield Court today. A part of the blue-brick capped garden wall is all that now remains of the property.

Sketch of Fern House taken from a share offer by James Fern Webster. c1880.

The census returns of 1881 record that Webster was living there with his wife Sabina, daughter Mary and son Frederick. Sabina passed away in 1888 and James was living at Edgbaston at that time. He lived to the age of 84 and was buried in a vault in St. James Churchyard in 1904.

By 1891 Fern House was occupied by Frederick Martino, a manufacturer from Sheffield, his wife Alice, Irene his daughter and two servants. Kelly's Directory of 1892 referred to 'Martino Patent Steel Tool Manufacturing Co.' which may have operated in Solihull Lodge, and to which he may have been connected.

At this time Thomas Bourne, a mechanic's draughtsman, was living in Heath House. He and his wife Alice had three sons and four daughters and employed one servant, who lived in.

Around 1881 Heath House was unoccupied and it was probably at this time that an advertisement by Grimly and Sons was produced which provided details of the size and style of the property. This described the building as containing:

> '.... Spacious Entrance Hall, Dining Room, Drawing Room, Breakfast Room, China and Cooks Pantries, Kitchen and Cellars. On the first floor; Five chambers, Dressing Room, Store Closet, W.C. and Laundry. Second floor; Four Bedrooms and Store Closet.... Outside stables for two horses and a Carriage House'.

The grounds included a kitchen garden and pleasure grounds which would have been laid out in the area which is now occupied by Shenstone Court.

A second advertisement, probably published by Webster, sought investors for various patents but it also included a statement that the house was:

> '....situated in a healthy neighbourhood...' ......

Both advertisements carried a sketch of the front facade of the houses, which was designed in a Gothic style.

Constructed mainly of the 'best blue Staffordshire bricks' the property was lit by gas and it is believed that many important visitors to J.F. Webster's nearby aluminium factory were entertained there by his wife Sabina.

Many of the houses and cottages which provided accommodation during the reign of Queen Victoria were demolished a long time ago. This was the case with three cottages which were located alongside the canal between the High Street Bridge and the boundary with Yardley Wood, one of which was the beerhouse discussed in a previous chapter.

The lack of accurate addresses in the Census Enumerators Books, except for principal houses such as Colebrook Priory and Warren House, make it virtually impossible to accurately locate the houses of the Victorian period. In 1881 more detailed information was provided and it is possible to locate and discover some of the dwellings which still exist today. Information about them is scarce and I, therefore, simply list them below:

Peterbrook Road:

Highfield Cottage; occupied by Alfred Bucknell, Qualified Teacher, his wife Selina, 3 daughters 2 sons and his mother.

Victorian Cottages in Peterbrook Road near its junction with High Street as they are today. 1995.

Mereside; two families are listed as occupying this cottage;
firstly Edward Payne, bricklayer and his wife Charlotte.
secondly Alfred Tonks, carriage folding step maker, his wife Eliza, 2 sons and 4 daughters.

Rose Cottage; Edward Leach, caretaker and his wife Mary.

High Street:

Peacock Cottage; near to the Prince of Wales Public House, home of Henry Higham, groom and coachman, wife Susanna, 2 daughters and a son.

Mona Cottage; at the corner of Aqueduct Road and High Street, William A. Barnes, bottle merchant, wife Clara, son, sister-in-law and servant.

Primrose Cottage; situated opposite 'Sunhaven' occupied in 1900 by Joseph W.P. Pittam.

Rose Bank can still be found in Aqueduct Road near to Mill Lodge School but it has been much modernised over the years. In 1881 it was the home of the Smith family whose three daughters and a son were looked after by the housekeeper because their parents were away from home on the night of the census.

ALUMINIUM WORKS

In 1877 James Fern Webster a mechanical and gas engineer who was living at Fern House had a factory, called Hollywood Works, built by the canal bridge in the High Street at a cost of £50,000. His company traded under the names of 'The Warwickshire Crown Metal Works' and 'Websters Patent Aluminium Crown Metal Co. Ltd'. The factory was described in an advertisement as having 'a canal frontage of forty yards on the "Birmingham and London Navigation" for easy transportation of goods'.

Almost all of the available information about Webster has been provided by members of his family, especially his great grandson the late Robert Shaw. He is reputed to have invented and developed the first process which enabled aluminium to be produced at an economic cost. A certain amount of evidence is available to support this claim at both Solihull Reference Library and Birmingham Science Museum. Probably the most significant evidence is provided by Webster's application dated 29th. November, 1879 for Letters Patent for the invention of 'A new or improved method of producing Aluminium Bronze'.

Information contained on a surviving business card confirms that twelve types of metal or metal alloy were produced at the Solihull Lodge Factory. These included Aluminium, Aluminium Silver Alloys, Silver Alloys and Aluminium Blue. There is also evidence which suggests that he produced five qualities of metal given a value between 1 and 5, the hardest was adapted for use for castings and the softest for wire and tubes. Each grade of metal would have been marked with the appropriate stamp.

The factory in Solihull Lodge was not his only base. An advertisement listed another works 'Heeley Mills, Sheffield'. The same advertisement confirmed his head office as being 34 St. Mary Axe, London EC with branch offices at Broad Street, Birmingham and Heeley Mills, Sheffield. A second advertisement, however, contained different addresses, the London Office being 34 Leadnhall Street and a foundry at Park Street, Southwark. On this occasion there is no mention of works or offices at Sheffield. Unfortunately neither of these advertisements is dated and we are not able, therefore, to even surmise when he was operating at these premises.

Copy of trade stamp which was used to stamp Websters Aluminium products. This one was used to denote grade 3 soft aluminium. c1880.

Copy of a visiting card which names Hollywood Works in Solihull Lodge.

NON-OXIDISATION.

WEBSTER'S PATENT
ALUMINIUM METALS.

REGISTERED

TRADE MARK.

LONDON OFFICES:
34, LEADENHALL STREET, E.C.

FOUNDRY:
PARK STREET, SOUTHWARK.

WORKS:
SOLLIHULL LODGE, near BIRMINGHAM

BIRMINGHAM OFFICES:
BROAD STREET

Medal of the First Class.

GLASGOW, 1888.

Sole Manufacturers:

THE ALUMINIUM CROWN METAL CO., LIMITED.

BRILLIANCY. — CONDUCTIVITY. — DUCTILITY. — DURABILITY.

TENSILE STRENGTH.

Copy of advertisement for Websters products.

The works at Solihull Lodge comprised of a casting shop, refinery and joiners shops, two large shops, metal warehouse, storerooms and offices. The appliances, furnaces and machinery were said to have been designed by Webster. When he offered it for lease it was advertised as being stocked with 'fourteen tons of the best Aluminium Bronzes, best and common German silver and other Alloy'.

It is surprising that throughout the period that the Aluminium Works was operating none of the census returns record any one who was employed in an occupation relating to the metal industry.

Webster patented more than two hundred inventions during his lifetime, the diversity of which was demonstrated in an entry in the Birmingham Industrial Exhibition catalogue of 1865. The entry confirms his exhibition included 'Specimens of flat chain, suitable for mail and other purposes; smelting furnace for refining iron and zinc; Oxyhydrogen blow pipe; lighthouse lamp to burn oil and oxygen; regulator valve for water or gas; nail twisting machine etc. by James Webster'. The entry was listed under the categories of 'articles manufactured or in the process of manufacture in the ordinary way of business' and secondly as 'new inventions or original contrivances to economise labour or time'. His specifications for these and other products are held at Birmingham Science Museum and Solihull Reference Library.

Available evidence suggests that he exhibited far and wide. An article in the Birmingham Daily Mail dated 30th. October, 1883 stated 'Last night upwards of twenty tons of various kinds of goods made from Websters Aluminium Metal, produced at the works of the Crown Metal Aluminium Company, Solihull Lodge, were consigned to the Calcutta Exhibition'.

It has been claimed that the Prime Minister, Lord Salisbury and the Right Honourable Arthur Balfour visited the works. Webster retired in 1887 and was said to have received payment in the sum of £240,000 for his patents, works and plant from a Mr. Cavner.

Webster went to live at Heath House, Edgbaston where he died in 1904. An obituary in the Daily Chronicle dated 2nd. November, 1904 read 'Mr. James Fern Webster, the pioneer of the Aluminium Industry, died in Birmingham yesterday, aged 84'.

All remaining evidence of the works disappeared when it was purchased in 1911 for demolition by Mr. Vaux, a builder.

*The demolition of Hollywood Works c1911.
This appears to be the only photographic evidence of
the works which is available but it gives us an idea
of the size and style of the building.*

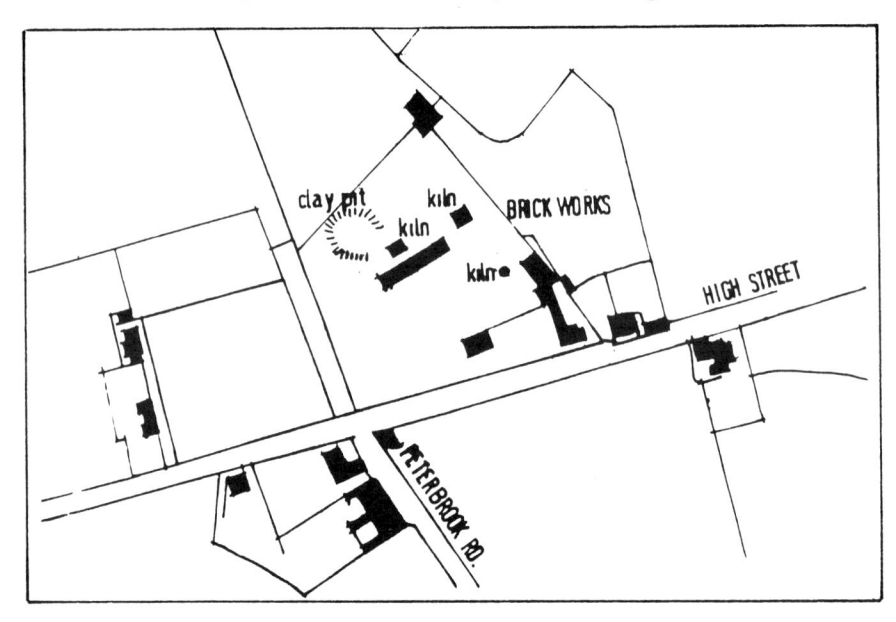

*Plan of Brickworks showing two square and one circular kiln.
Based on O.S. Map 1883 with the kind permission of
Ordnance Survey.*

LOCAL BRICKWORKS

During the nineteenth century brickworks tended to be established wherever there were sufficient deposits of clay and a lack of natural building materials such as stone. Early ordnance survey maps indicate several old clay pits in Solihull Lodge.

The existence of a brick manufacturing industry in the area was recorded as early as 1806 when the Rate Book of that year informs us that John Ballard had a brick-kiln but its exact location is unknown.

The available evidence suggests that there were brickworks in the area which had, over a period of time, closed down. This is supported by entries in the Tythe Apportionment of 1837 which refers to fields as 'Roughland used to be a brick-kiln', 'part of brick-kiln pits' and 'brick-kiln piece'.

The same document informs us that there were two brickworks situated opposite Peterbrook Road. Humphry Poutney occupied a 'brick-kiln' whilst James Payton occupied a 'brick yard, half spoil, half clear land'. Both pieces of land were in the area of Greenslade Road and both appear to have been operating as brickworks at that time.

It is clear that the kiln operated by Humphry Poutney ceased to operate as it is not shown on subsequent maps. The brick yard worked by James Payton in 1841 continued to manufacture bricks until well into the twentieth century.

The brickworks had its own clay pit and comprised three kilns, two rectangular ones and a circular one. Circular kilns had been developed because they provided a more even distribution of heat than their rectangular predecessors and thus produced a product of better quality.

There were sixteen men who described themselves as brickmakers living in the area between 1841 and 1900. It is not possible, however, to determine from the available records whether they were employed at the Solihull Lodge Brickworks or at a second works which was situated just over the boundary with Worcestershire in Maypole Lane. Many of the names just disappear from the records as the century progresses and we can only assume that they left the area. We are, however, able to trace others.

David Clark was recorded as a brickmaker in 1841. Ten years later his wife Mary Ann was described as a widow with five children, the youngest John only ten months old. It seems reasonable to assume that David had died sometime within the two years preceding the 1851 census.

Others stopped brickmaking to take up alternative careers. Peter Juggins, for example, a brickmaker in 1851/61 had by 1871 become a beerhouse keeper whilst William Houghton became a farmer. Solomon Cox a brick labourer in 1871 had become an agricultural labourer by 1881 whilst ten years later his brother Thomas had entered the industry as a brickmaker.

The available evidence suggests that the last known brickmaker to operate the Solihull Lodge Brickworks was John Loughton, a brick and tile manufacturer, and he was probably the one who took the business into the twentieth century.

THE SOLIHULL LODGE COMMUNITY

The size of the community in Solihull Lodge in 1841 was one-hundred and ninety-seven souls. It slowly increased to reach a figure of two-hundred and sixty-seven in 1891. During the same period the number of households grew from a low of forty-six to a high of sixty in 1881. Ten years later the number had reduced to fifty-seven.

What is probably more interesting from an historical point of view, however, is the size and composition of the households, a subject which has long been of interest to historians. For many years the popular conception has been of large Victorian families. Recent research, however, has shown that large families were not as common as was once thought.

In the case of Solihull Lodge the size of the average nuclear family was small. In 1851 and 1891 the majority of families only had two children whilst in the intervening years most only had one child. It is true that there were larger families, some with as many as seven or eight children, but these were the exception rather than the rule.

The number of extended families in the area remained fairly constant throughout the period. The creation of these families was often brought about by the provision of support for elderly parents or in-laws, widowed sisters or brothers, nephews, neices or grandchildren.

Household sizes followed a similar pattern to that of the family generally ranging from between two and five people. Again there were a few larger households, some comprising as many as eight, nine or ten people.

One factor which appears to have had a distinct bearing on nineteenth century life was the ownership of property. The majority of the population during this period leased rather than owned the property in which they lived, or worked. This allowed the population to move from place to place with ease. The most commonly used means of measuring these migratory patterns is the distance people travelled from their place of birth.

When this method is applied to the families who settled at various times in Solihull Lodge, it shows there were considerable differences between the distances travelled by men and by women. Whilst the majority of males were moving within a radius of about five miles of their birthplace, their wives had often travelled far greater distances, in some cases in excess of thirty miles. Some of the young women may have met and married local men whilst in service.

One of the main reasons for families moving around was the need to find work. This was demonstrated in Solihull Lodge where almost all of those employed making needles left the area when the industry ceased to operate. Possibly one of the most mobile groups of workers during this period was that of servants, which was also a major form of employment. Servants stayed in the area for less than ten years. The exception was Harriet Harcox, a domestic servant employed by the Kendrick family for most of the second half of the nineteenth century.

The number of families employing servants in Solihull Lodge increased during the period reaching a peak of nineteen in 1881. As a general rule it has always been thought that the employment of servants was the prerogative of the rich, but in this community some were employed by agricultural labourers, who were on the same step of the social ladder as themselves.

Both males and females appear to have entered service at a young age. Throughout the period the majority of those employed in Solihull Lodge were aged between fourteen and twenty-five. The youngest recorded was just eleven years old.

Not all families were continually moving however. There were some who remained in the area for the whole of the Victorian period.

Richard Blythe, a farmer, appeared in the Census of 1841 with his wife Letitia, one son and two daughters. Ten years later his family had increased to three sons and four daughters. Richard owned land adjacent to the canal but it is not clear if this was all or part of the twenty-nine acres he is recorded as farming in 1861. The acreage of his land had increased by the date of the next census to forty and a half acres enabling him to employ a man and a boy.

His son Richard married in 1854 and had two sons and four daughters. Like his father he was a farmer and he remained in the district for the rest of the century. By contrast another son George married in 1867 and moved away from the area to set up home.

One of his daughters, Letitia, died in 1869 at the age of thirty two leaving her nine year old son, Charles, to be brought up by his grandparents.

By 1881 Richard's son William had a household of his own which included his sister Ann, who was widowed, and a nephew and niece.

Richard senior died at the age of seventy five in 1879 whilst his wife, Letitia, died two years later at the age of seventy four. Both were buried at St. James Church in Shirley.

Of particular interest is the family of John and Ann Juggins because most of their children remained in the area after they left home.

In 1841 John, a fifty year old agricultural labourer, and his wife Ann had six sons living with them.

John occupied land which skirted the High Street and Peterbrook Road some of which he owned himself whilst some was in the ownership of Solihull Charity Estates. He probably lived in a house situated at the corner of High Street and Peterbrook Road. John appears to have climbed the social ladder describing himself as a farmer in 1851 and ten years later was able to employ a servant. By the date of the 1871 census he had a daughter, Alice, and was the employer of three men.

John's son William, a needle pointer in 1851, set up home in the area with his wife Sarah, who was also a needle maker. They had a son and a daughter and when the needle mill closed down William turned to agricultural labouring to earn a living and Sarah was working as a laundress. By the 1881 census they had either left the area or died.

John's son Ambrose was also living in the area at this time with his wife Elizabeth and one year old daughter Alice Elizabeth, as was his son Thomas and his wife Emma who remained in the area until 1891. They had no children of their own but in 1881 their household included a three year old nurse child, James Knight and Thomas Knight who was described as a nephew. Emma died in 1892.

Another son, Peter, was a brick maker in 1861 but by 1871 he had taken over as landlord of the Prince of Wales Public House. Peter and his wife Mary had five daughters and two sons. By 1891 Peter had died and his wife Mary, assisted by her daughter Florence, ran the pub, at the same time as running a farm.

A second family headed by an Ambrose Juggins appears in the records in 1871. Ambrose, also an agricultural labourer, and his wife Caroline had been living in Derbyshire. They had four daughters and six sons. There is no evidence to connect this family with the other Juggins living in the area and it is quite possible that their arrival was just a coincidence.

All communities in the nineteenth century conformed to a social structure or class system. The upper class of the area were the Chattocks, Kendricks, Bamptons and Websters. Farmers fitted into the system depending on the acreage of their farms.

The Blythe family would have occupied a position in the social hierarchy of the area which we would today refer to as middle class. On the other hand Northampton born Thomas Clayton, who is first recorded in 1871, and described as a travelling tinker, would have been positioned at the bottom of the social scale. He would have earned his living as a mender of pots, kettles and pans.

His wife Mary came from Lapworth and they had five children the eldest of which, thirteen year old Sarah, was born in Shirley. It appears that Thomas and Mary lived for some time in Tanworth as the remainder of their children were born there. It is also worthy of note that at this time another Tinker from Northampton, Joseph Clayton, possibly Thomas' father, also lived in the area with his wife Patience, who was blind.

When they were living in Solihull Lodge Mary and Thomas were recorded as occupying a 'Railway Carriage by the Drawbridge'. The nearest railway line at this time was the Birmingham to Solihull line situated a considerable distance away. How the carriage came to be in the area is a mystery. It can only be surmised that it was transported to the drawbridge along the canal, but for what reason is unknown.

By 1876 Mary had given birth to two more sons and Thomas had, at the age of thirty nine, passed away. The 1881 census shows that Mary still had five of her children living with her. Sarah had left home, quite possibly to go into service. Mary earned her living as a charwoman with two of her sons contributing to the family income by working as agricultural labourers. The family home was still in the Drawbridge area but we do not know for certain whether or not they occupied the Railway Carriage.

At this time Mary's sister, Teresa, who was a hawker or travelling pedlar of small wares was also living with her. It may have been that she joined her sister to support her when she was widowed.

Ten years later Mary's household had become smaller, Teresa had moved on leaving only sons Thomas, William, Joseph and Walter living at home.

In 1894 William at the age of twenty seven married Alice Willis from Yardley Wood at St. James Church, Shirley.

Throughout the nineteenth century it was agriculture which provided a living for the majority of the Solihull Lodge community. Some historians suggest that during this period agriculture ceased to be the country's major source of employment becoming just an industry among other industries. This is supported in Solihull Lodge by the more varied and diverse occupations of individuals we find recorded in the 1891 census. For example there is a teacher, a chemist, an engine driver and a spectacle maker. It can only be assumed that people following these trades were travelling into nearby Birmingham to earn a living.

All communities require various facilities to provide for their needs such as food, clothing, education, worship and also somewhere to relax. Not all of these amenities were provided within the boundaries of the area but all were within walking distance.

There is a lack of accurate information available which confirms the number and location of shops which served the area during the Victorian period. The little information we do have suggests that shops were opened and closed in various locations throughout the period.

We do know that in 1806 there were three shops, one of them a grocers, but by 1837, the date of the Tythe, there was only one. This was owned by William Lindon and situated in Yardley Wood Road close to the Birmingham boundary. There was still only one recorded in 1846 owned by Thomas Vale but it appears his property was situated at the corner of Priory Road and Colebrook Road.

The only definite location we possess dates from 1871 when Henry Mansill was described as a grocer living at the 'Drawbridge Stores'. A shop was located here and run by Edmund Field his wife and servants in 1891. He earned a living as a grocer, coal dealer and farmer. The Drawbridge Stores continued to trade well into the twentieth century.

Some services were provided by individuals working out of their homes. Ladies dress requirements were well catered for as dressmakers appear on every census. In 1861 there were as many as four. Two of them, Mary Mace and Eliza Shipton both lived in the area for at least ten years.

An interesting entry in the census return of 1881 concerns twenty year old Lydia Crockford and her fifteen year old brother Alfred. They are described as Drapers and Grocers, but it is not clear whether or not they had a shop in the area. The most interesting aspect of their entry, however, is that Lydia was born in Nova Scotia, North America. Her brother gives his place of birth as Birmingham which suggests that she had lived in England from an early age.

It has always been believed that religion was important to Victorians but it is clear than in some cases babies were only baptised if they were not expected to survive.

There were two churches within travelling distance of the area, St. James the Great in Shirley and Christ Church, Yardley Wood. There is ample evidence available to confirm that St. James was used for weddings, baptisms and funerals.

Christ Church was the closer of the two and is most likely the one to which Webster referred in his advertisement when he described Fern House as being 'within ten minutes walk from a Church of England'.

The Tythe of 1837 stated that Samuel Guest owned a cottage, garden and site of a meeting house in Yardley Wood Road adjacent to the boundary with Birmingham.

During the century a mission Church was established by St. James with services every Sunday afternoon. It is possible that this was the mission shown on the 1904 Ordnance Survey map in Yardley Wood Road.

In 1883 a school was established in Shirley, by St. James Church to teach the under twelves and soon after a new one was built. It was rebuilt in 1852. There is every likelihook that many of the children from the Solihull Lodge area attended this school but I have not found any evidence to support this. Alternatively some may have attended the mission in Yardley Wood Road which may also have served as a school. There is a school marked on the 1883 map in the same position. Other scholars may have attended Yardley Wood School.

The number of children described as scholars, in the Census Returns rises from a figure of sixteen in 1851 to forty eight in 1881. They were generally aged between four and thirteen years although as the century progressed there were one or two older children, of fourteen and fifteen recorded as being scholar. As a general rule however, as soon as a child was able he or she was expected to contribute to the family income.

The Education Acts of the 1870s saw the creation of school boards and made education compulsory up to the age of ten years. School fees at this time were between 1d and 3d a week. It was not until the 1890s that free education was introduced.

School records appear to suggest that children were in poor health as they were often absent from school because of illness. If the truth be known, however, they were more likely kept at home to help on the farm.

There is only one teacher recorded as living in the area, in 1891. Forty year old Alfred Bucknall was described as a 'certified teacher'. He originated from Madeley in Shropshire. He lived at Highfield Cottage in Peterbrook Road with his wife Selina, sons Thomas and Reginald, and daughters Madeleine, Lilian and Eveline. He also had his widowed mother, aged sixty nine, living with him.

The only evidence of scholars receiving a higher education appears in the 1881 census when Earnest Chattock was described as an Oxford Undergraduate.

The only places for relaxation were Public Houses or, as they were sometimes known, Beerhouses. Other than the Beerhouse at Pear Tree Farm and the Drawbridge which I have discussed in an earlier chapter there was also the Prince of Wales Public House.

The Prince of Wales Public House is first mentioned in the census returns of 1871 when Peter Juggins was the landlord. Peter lived there with his wife Mary, daughter Mary Ann and sons George and Walter. The household at this time also contained a lodger Hannah Lea.

Sketch of the original Prince of Wales Public House

Peter and Mary had four other daughters, one of whom helped her mother to run the pub after Peter's death sometime between 1881 and 1891.

Mary Ann had left home by 1881. We can only speculate that she had either married or left to seek employment. George and Walter were both agricultural labourers and they lived at home until 1881 and 1891 respectively.

One of the main sources describing the original Prince of Wales is an article in the Solihull News dated 13th. March, 1954. The original building was located on the same parcel of land as the present public house.

The original double fronted building stood much closer to the High Street than today's building. In Victorian times of course car parking provision was not a consideration. It is believed that it was a coaching inn with stables at the rear.

The newspaper article is an interview with a Mrs. Martha Wedge who described the building's interior as it was in 1905 when she and her husband took over the pub. Customers sat on old barrels and cases drinking by the light produced by thirteen oil lamps. She also said that customers maintained the old custom of using three handled quart tankards which they passed around for 'communial sips'. A water pump was positioned at the front of the building.

The premises were modernised in around 1924 before the original building was demolished in the late 1950s and replaced with the building we see today.

Primrose Cottage, 1995.

INTO THE TWENTIETH CENTURY

Solihull Lodge experienced very little change in the period between 1901 and the 1950s. Industrial activities were on the decline and it remained a farming area. A small number of dwellings were erected together with a small shopping centre in Prince of Wales Lane. From the end of the Second World War, however, the area rapidly grew into the suburban sprawl we know today.

All of the industrial buildings and, with the exception of Colebrook Priory, the large houses have been demolished at different times to clear the way for new development.

The number of dwellings increased dramatically and today are comprised of houses, flats and maisonettes. There is also a home for the elderly situated on the High Street. This vast increase in properties has been accompanied by a corresponding increase in the number of roads.

Such a large increase in the population has inevitably resulted in the provision of other facilities such as schools and shops. A second shopping centre was constructed in Oxhill Road as part of the residential development of that area.

Today's primary school children are able to attend one of the two schools in the area, Peterbrook School in the High Street or Mill Lodge School in Aqueduct Road. Peterbrook School alone provides education for over four hundred children.

The development of the area has also seen the arrival of other facilities which serve the community. A purpose built Community Centre has been constructed in Grafton Road and a Doctors Practice has also been established in Grafton Road.

Possibly the greatest change which has taken place since the nineteenth century is that generally speaking people no longer work in the area but travel either into Birmingham, Solihull or even further. This has resulted in an immense increase in road traffic and the improvement of the road system, vastly different from the leafy lanes of the nineteenth century.

BIBLIOGRAPHY

BOOKS

Bates Sue. **Shirley, A Pictorial History.** Phillimore 1993.

Booth D.T.N. **Warwickshire Watermills.** Midland Wind and Watermills Group, 1978.

Burman J. **Gleanings of Warwickshire History.** 1933.

Burman J. **Shirley and its Church.** Revised edition 1968.

Dugdale W. **The Antiquities of Warwickshire, Vol. II.** 1730.

Ekwall E. **Dictionary of English Place Names,** 1960 - 4th Edition.

Hadfield C. and Norris J. **Waterways to Stratford.** David & Charles 2nd Edition 1968.

Horn P. **The Victorian and Edwardian School Child.** Alan Sutton 1989.

Huggett F.E. **A Day in the life of a Victorian Farm Worker.** George Allen & Unwin Ltd 1972.

Jones J. Morris. **Walks in Yardley Wood.** Unpublished transcript, Yardley Wood Library.

Jones J. Morris. **Watermills of the Cole and Blythe Valleys.** Unpublished transcript. Hall Green Library.

Field Studies in the West Midlands Vol. 1. The Geographical Association (Birmingham Branch) 1968.

Seaby Wilfred A. **Windmills in Warwickshire.** Warwickshire Museums Publications 1979.

Shaw Robert. **The Silver Pimpernel.** Unpublished transcript, Solihull Library.

Skipp V. **Medieval Yardley.** Phillimore 1970.

Victoria County History of Warwickshire Vol I & Vol III.

Victoria County History of Worcestershire Vol. III

Woodall J. **The Book of Greater Solihull.** Barracuda Books 1990.

DOCUMENTS

Census Enumerators Books for Shirley, Solihull 1841-1891. Solihull Reference Library.

Directories of Solihull and District 1835-1916 Warwick Record Office.

History of Shirley; Shirley Womens Institute 1956. Solihull Reference Library.

Indentures referring to Colebrook Priory; Mr & Mrs R. Hughes.

Inscriptions in St. James Churchyard, Shirley. Warwick Record Office.

Kellys Post Office Directories of Warwickshire. Solihull Reference Library.

St. James Church, Shirley, Parish Registers. Warwick Record Office.

Solihull Inclosure Award 1843. Warwick Record Office.

Solihull Tythe Apportionment 1837. Solihull Reference Library.

Solihull News. 24 February 1954 and 8 February 1958. Solihull Reference Library.

Solihull Rate Book. 1806. Solihull Reference Library.

White and Company. Directory of Warwickshire 3rd Edition. 1874.

Solihull Reference Library.

MAPS

A map of the Hemlingford Hundred. Henry Beighton 1725.

Solihull Tythe Map 1837.

1" O.S. Map of Solihull 1831.

1:2500 O.S. Map of Solihull 1883.

1:10560; 6" to the mile map of Solihull 1905 Survey.

1:2500 O.S. Map of Solihull 1904.

ACKNOWLEDGEMENTS

I wish to thank the following for their help whilst researching this book.

The Staff of Solihull Library, Local Studies Department, especially Mrs. Sue Bates for her guidance and support.

The Staff of Warwick County Records Office.

The Staff of Forge Needle Mill, Redditch.

Dr. J. Andrews of Birmingham Science Museum.

Mr. & Mrs. R. Hughes for allowing me access to documents relating to Colebrook Priory.

Mrs. Ballard for her memories and photographs of the area.

Mrs. Knight of Saint James School Shirley.

Finally I must thank my wife Brenda for her most valuable help during my research and the patience she has shown on the numerous occasions she has read the manuscript and offered her advice.

ILLUSTRATION ACKNOWLEDGEMENTS

The illustrations used in this book are reproduced by kind permission of:

Plates 1, 2, 4, 7 and 10 - Solihull Library.

Plates 6 and 8 - Shirley Womens Institute.

Plates 13, 15 and 16 - Birmingham Science Museum

Plate 11 - Mr. and Mrs. R. Hughes.

Plate 5 - Mrs. Ballard.

Plate 19 and cover picture - Brenda Adams.

All remaining illustrations are from the author's collection. Maps have been prepared by the author.

LOCAL HISTORY BOOKS
BIRMINGHAM AND DISTRICT

Birmingham Theatres	Victor J. Price	£10.95
Old Ladywood Remembered	Victor J. Price	£ 5.95
Aston Remembered	Victor J. Price	£ 5.95
The Bull Ring Remembered	Victor J. Price	£ 5.95
Birmingham Yesterday, It's People and Places	Victor J. Price	£14.95
Kings Norton - A History	Helen Goodger	£ 7.95
Memories of Old Ward End	Jose Jukes	£ 7.95
A Postcard from the Lickeys	Joe & Frances Brannan	£12.95
Birmingham's Jewellery Quarter	Alison Gledhill	£ 5.95
Sidelights on a City	Douglas V. Jones	£ 4.95
A Postcard from Bournville	Joe & Frances Brannan	£13.95
B.A.I. - The Birmingham Athletic Institute Remembered	(Ed) M. Irene-Waterman	£ 5.95
Handsworth Remembered	Victor J. Price	£ 5.95
Air Raids Over Yardley	John Abbott	£ 5.95
The Children's Home Village	Jill Plumley	£10.95
Balsall Heath - A History	Valerie M. Hart	£ 7.95
The Child's Vanishing Landscape (Listed Midland Buildings through the eyes of children)	(Ed) Sue Cooke	£ 9.95
Aston Villa on old cigarette and trade cards	Derrick Spinks	£ 6.95
Around 4 O'Clock (Memories of Sparkhill & Acocks Green)	Frances Wilmot	£ 8.95
Looking at Birmingham	Anny Richardson	£12.95
The Bournville Hallmark Housing People for 100 years	Judy Hillman	£ 4.95
Josiah Mason 1795 - 1881 Birmingham's Benevolent Benefactor	Brian Jones	£ 9.95
Harborne Remembered	Victor J. Price	£ 5.95
My Mother's Son - The Story of Lozells	Patrick Hughes	£ 6.95
Coseley - A Walk Back in Time	Beryl Wilkes	£ 8.95

LOCAL HISTORY BOOKS
WARWICKSHIRE AND WORCESTERSHIRE

Around Alcester in Old Photographs	Alcester & District LHS	£ 3.95
Portraits of a Lady (Countess of Warwick)	David Buttery	£ 3.95
St Mary's Church, Studley	(Ed) Harold Parker	£ 1.95
Sent From Coventry	Bud Paul	£12.00
Olton Heritage (Solihull)	Jean Powrie, Margaret Jordan & Carol Andrews	£ 6.95
Sixty Glorious Years in Bidford on Avon	Peggy Griffiths	£ 2.95
Damson By The Pound - Memories of a Warwickshire Family 1900-1939	Stanley Beavan	£11.95
Beneath The Great Elms (Whitnash)	Jean Field	£ 6.95
Henley-in-Arden - Life From The Past	Charles Welham	£ 7.95
She Dyed About Midnight (Warwick)	Jean Field	£ 7.95
Ullenhall (Life after Lady Luxborough)	Margaret Feeney	£ 6.95
Kings of Warwick (Hardback)	Jean Field	£18.00
Kings of Warwick (Paperback)	Jean Field	£ 9.95
Beauchamps (Rowney Green)	W. Eileen Davies	£ 7.95
Victorian Workhouse (Bromsgrove)	Neville Land	£ 7.95
The History of Redditch and the Locality	Neville Land	£ 6.95
Old Redditch - A Walk Back in Time	Lily Norris	£ 5.95

Available from all Midland booksellers or direct from the publisher:
(please enclose remittance and add 10% for postage)

BREWIN BOOKS
DORIC HOUSE, CHURCH STREET, STUDLEY, WARWICKSHIRE. B80 7LG
Tel: 01527 854228   Fax: 01527 852746